The ADVENTURES of DUKE

by **Ken Brady**

CERTIFIED THERAPY DOG

DUKE

Illustrated by **Jim Gross**

Briley & Baxter Publications | Plymouth, Massachusetts

Hardcover ISBN: 978-1-961978-13-3
Paperback ISBN: 978-1-961978-17-1

Book Design: Stacy A. Padula

Dedication

To Duke. What you have taught me about life cannot be measured. From you, I have learned what it means to be resilient, caring, loving, strong, and generous. Without you, there would be no book. Thank you for what you have done for me. You're always the best boy.

Also, to Rowan, Liam, Vivian, Lila, Bryson, and Nora, my beautiful grandchildren. This book is for you. Always remember I love you.

This is Duke.

Duke began his life on an island, where there were a lot of stray dogs.

A stray dog is one who doesn't have a home. Being a stray dog is hard.
There is no one to take care of you, no one to play with you,
no one to feed you, and no one to love you.

Life was hard for Duke. He was always hungry and thirsty because he had no food to eat or water to drink. He didn't even have a place to sleep!

Duke was lonely and sad, but most of all, he was scared.

Every day, Duke would
search for food. Sometimes,
a friendly person would give him
a leftover scrap or a sip of water. Duke always
appreciated it, but he was still hungry.

Each night, he had to sleep outside. This made him so nervous that he had trouble sleeping.

So, he wasn't just hungry and scared - he was tired too!

One day, a woman approached Duke. She bent down, touched his head, and told him she wanted to help him. Duke was scared and wasn't sure what to think, but he was so hungry and tired, he didn't have the energy to run away.

The woman picked Duke up and put him in her car. She brought him to a place with lots of other dogs.

She gave Duke food, water, and a soft blanket. Duke ate as much as he could. He felt so much better now that his belly was full. Then he lay down on his blanket and drifted off to sleep.

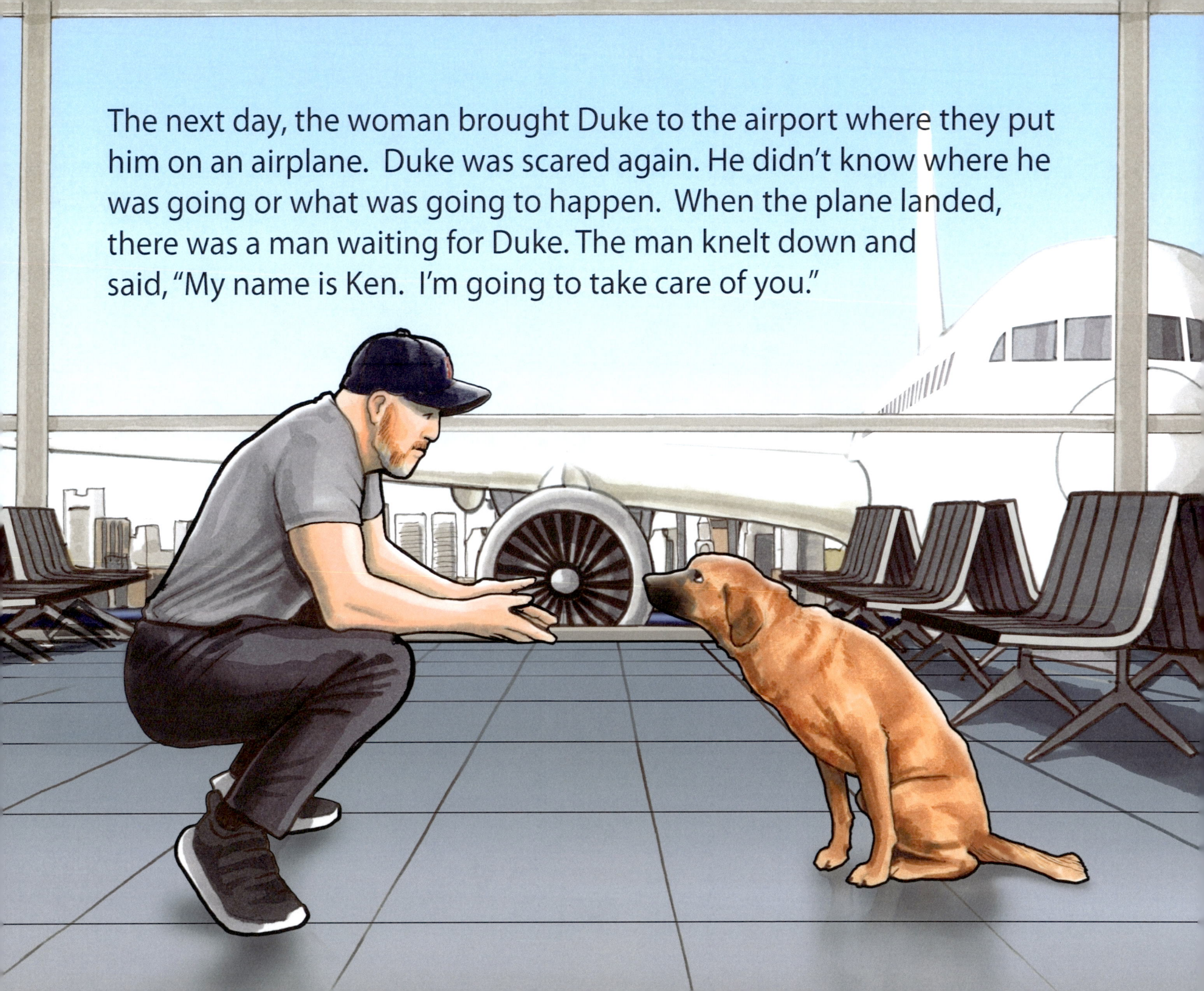

The next day, the woman brought Duke to the airport where they put him on an airplane. Duke was scared again. He didn't know where he was going or what was going to happen. When the plane landed, there was a man waiting for Duke. The man knelt down and said, "My name is Ken. I'm going to take care of you."

Together, they drove to Ken's house, where Ken showed Duke two bowls: "This one is for food, and this one is for water. These are yours now."

Ken took Duke to another room with a bed that had lots of chew toys and stuffed animals on it. Ken told Duke, "This is your bed. You can sleep here every night."

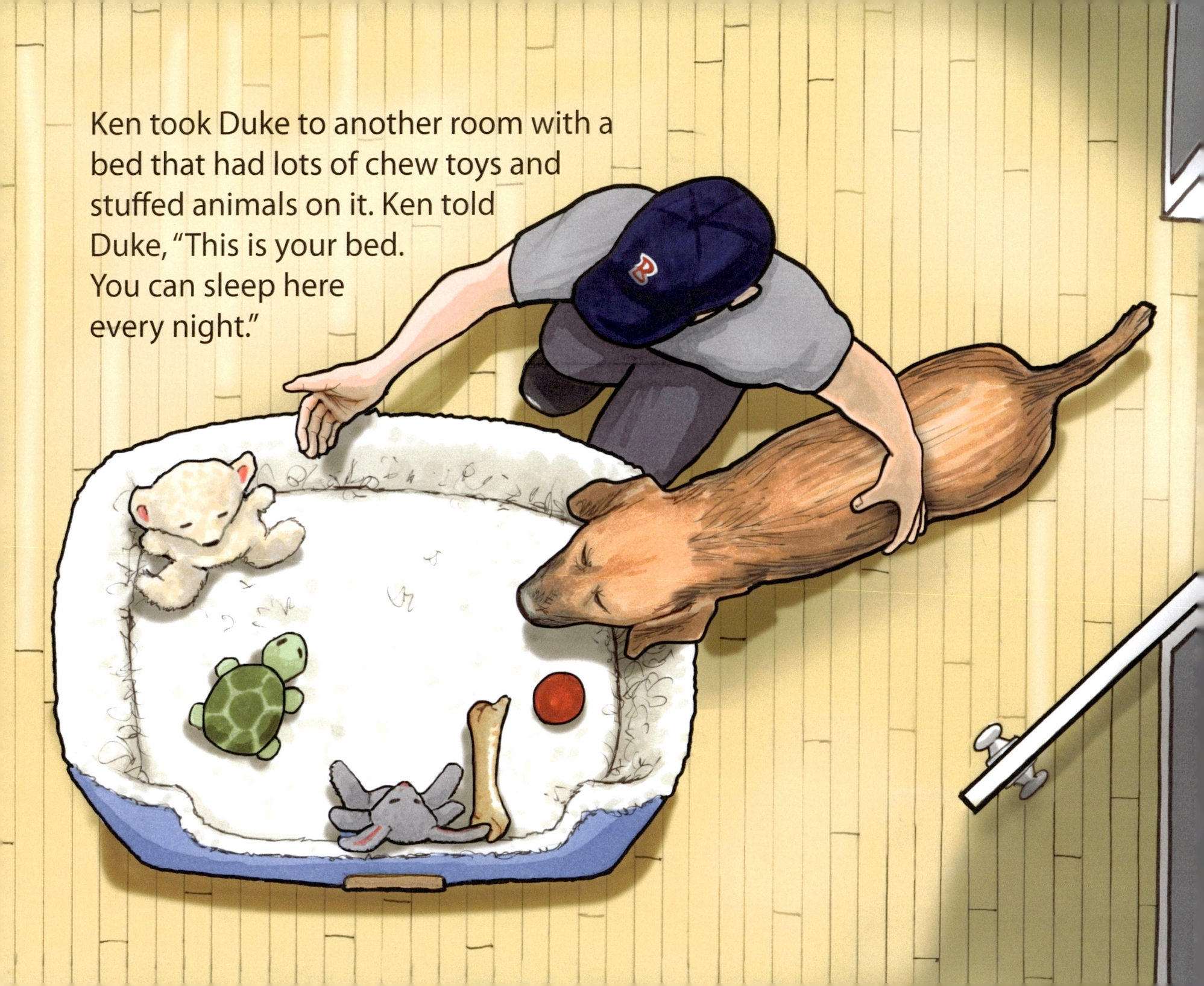

Duke could hardly believe it! After eating a big bowl of food and drinking some water, Duke lay down in his brand new, comfy bed, surrounded by his stuffed animals, and went to sleep.

The next day, Ken taught Duke how to sit, lie down, and roll over. Duke was so happy to have a home now that he worked really hard to master all his new skills.

Eventually Duke got so good at his skills that he could do them perfectly.

Duke was so happy to be a part of Ken's family.
He loved everyone, and they loved him.

Ken noticed that Duke had a positive effect on everyone he met. He would lean up against people so they could pet him, and he would cuddle up to the kids when they were having a bad day.

Everywhere Duke went, people felt better after spending time with him, so Ken got an idea...

Ken told Duke they were going to take a test, and it was very important. During the test, Duke performed all his new skills perfectly and passed! He was now an official therapy dog!

A therapy dog is a dog who helps people when they are dealing with difficult times in their lives.

If anyone knew about dealing with difficult times, it was Duke!

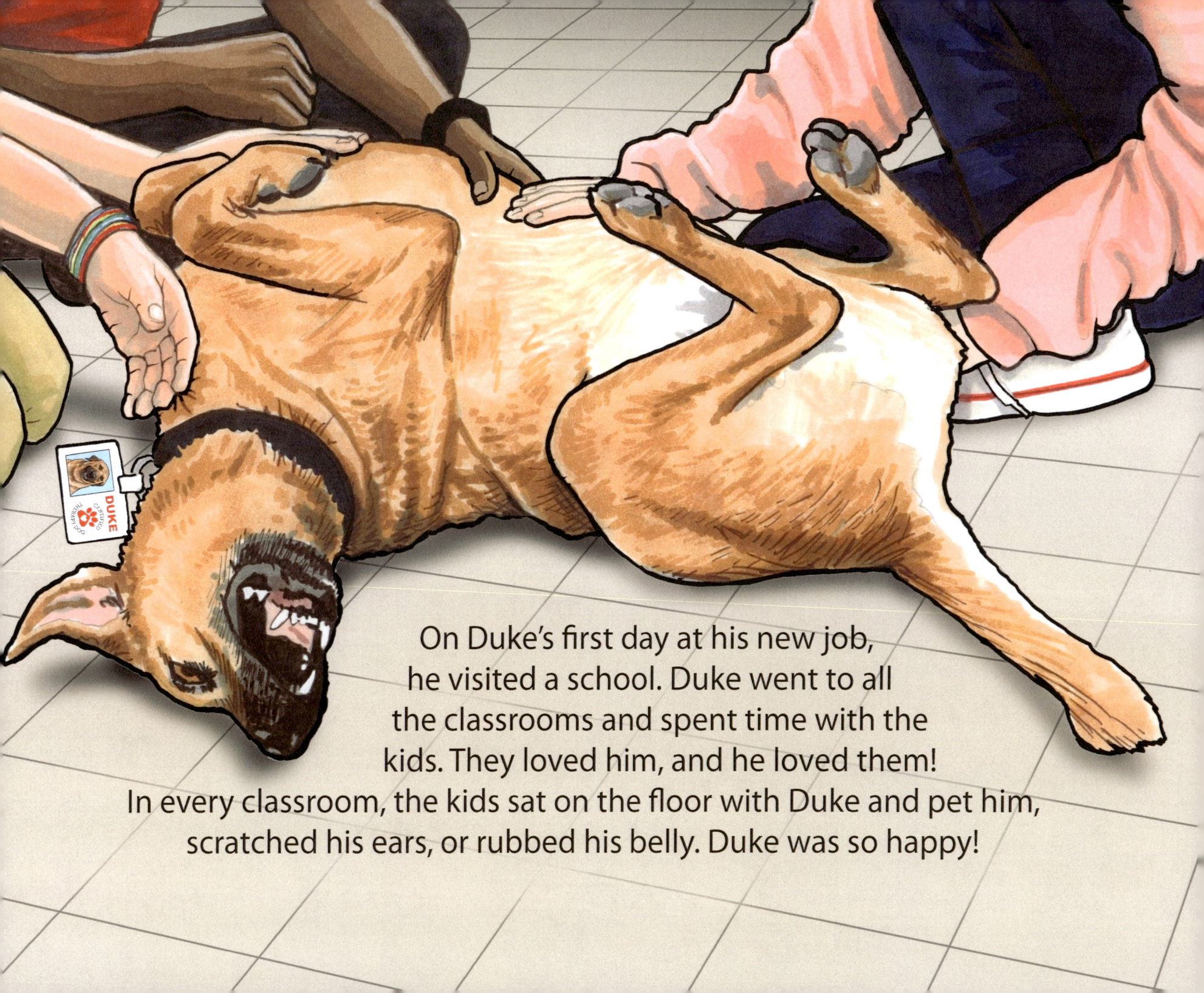

On Duke's first day at his new job,
he visited a school. Duke went to all
the classrooms and spent time with the
kids. They loved him, and he loved them!
In every classroom, the kids sat on the floor with Duke and pet him,
scratched his ears, or rubbed his belly. Duke was so happy!

After visiting all the classrooms, Duke went outside where the kids were having recess. Most of the kids were playing and having fun.

Duke noticed one little girl sitting all alone. She wasn't playing with anyone. She looked lonely.

Duke remembered what it was like to feel lonely, and he didn't want anyone to feel that way.

He picked up a ball and dropped it in front of the girl. She threw the ball, and Duke ran after it. Once he got the ball, he ran back to the girl and dropped it at her feet.

She threw the ball again, and when Duke brought it back to her, she smiled widely

Some of the other kids saw and said, "I want to throw the ball, too!"

Suddenly, all the kids were taking turns throwing the ball for Duke, having so much fun.

When it was time to leave, Duke looked back and saw the little girl smiling and talking to the other kids. She wasn't lonely anymore.

Duke had done his job.

A few days later, Ken took Duke to the park. They brought some sandwiches and snacks so they could have a picnic.

While they were there, Duke saw a woman and her son sitting on a bench. As people walked by, the woman asked them for money or food. Some people gave her a few coins, but most walked by without helping her.

Duke remembered what it was like to be hungry, and he didn't want anyone to feel that way. He picked up his and Ken's basket of sandwiches and brought it to the woman and her son.

They thanked Duke and ate until
they were full and happy!

Duke had done his job.

Another day, Duke visited a hospital. He went to a lot of different rooms to visit the patients. He knew they weren't feeling well and wanted to make them smile. All of their faces lit up with glee when they saw Duke!

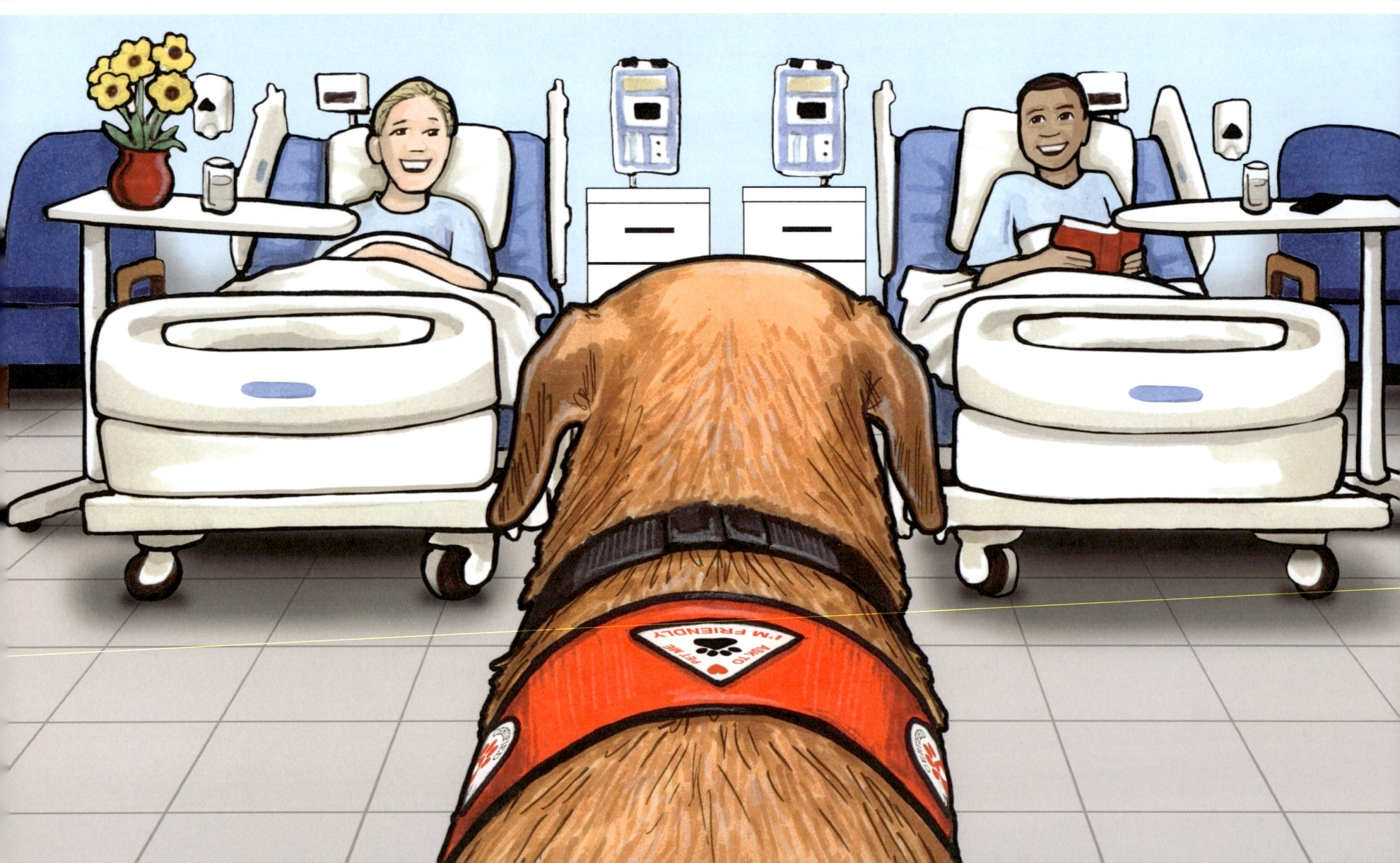

In one room, a little boy was lying in his bed with lots of wires and machines attached to him. He was about to have an operation, and he was scared. Duke remembered what it was like to be scared, and he didn't want anyone to feel that way.

Duke hopped up on the boy's bed, curled up beside him, and laid his head in the boy's lap. Smiling, the boy gently patted Duke's head and scratched his ears.

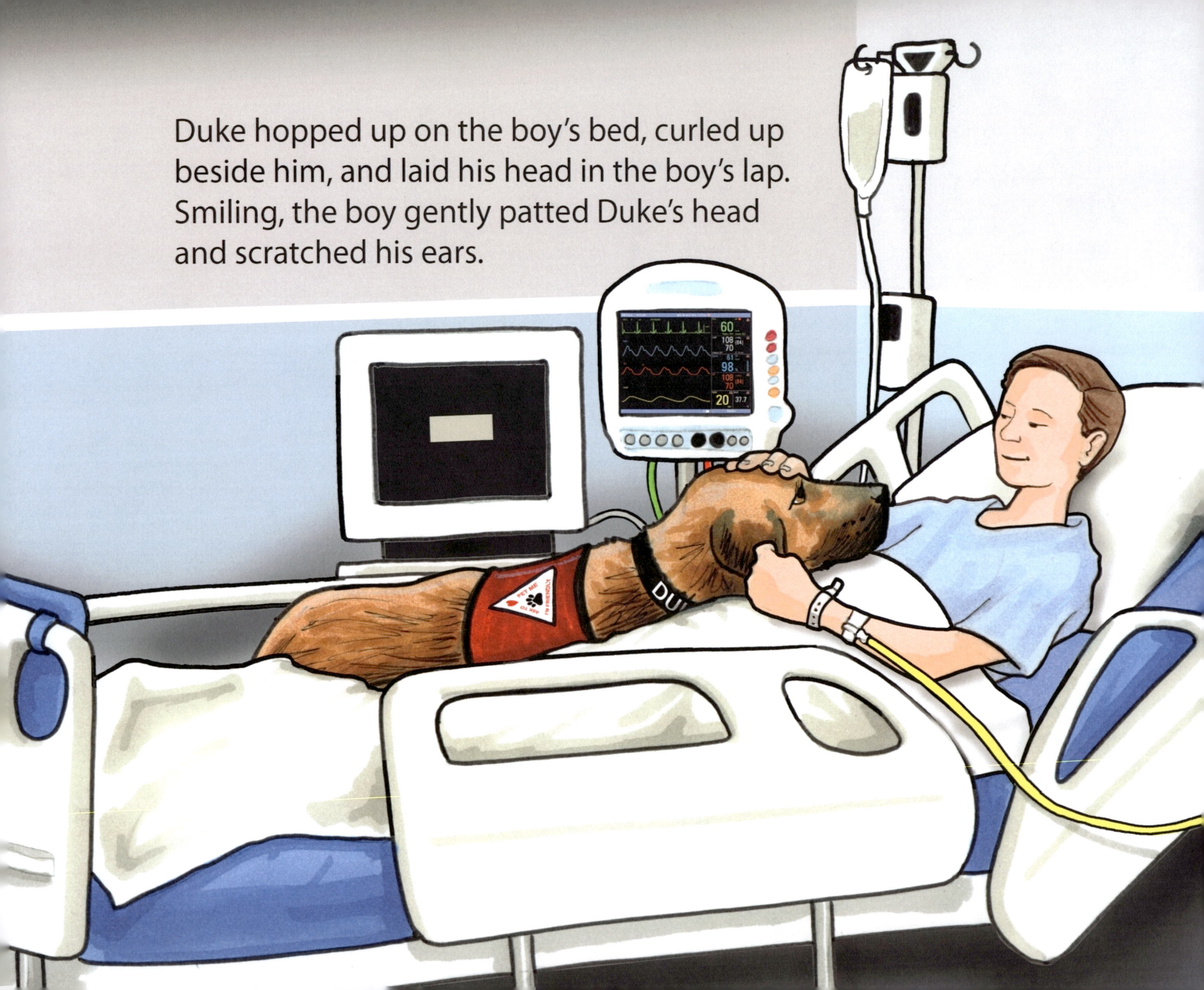

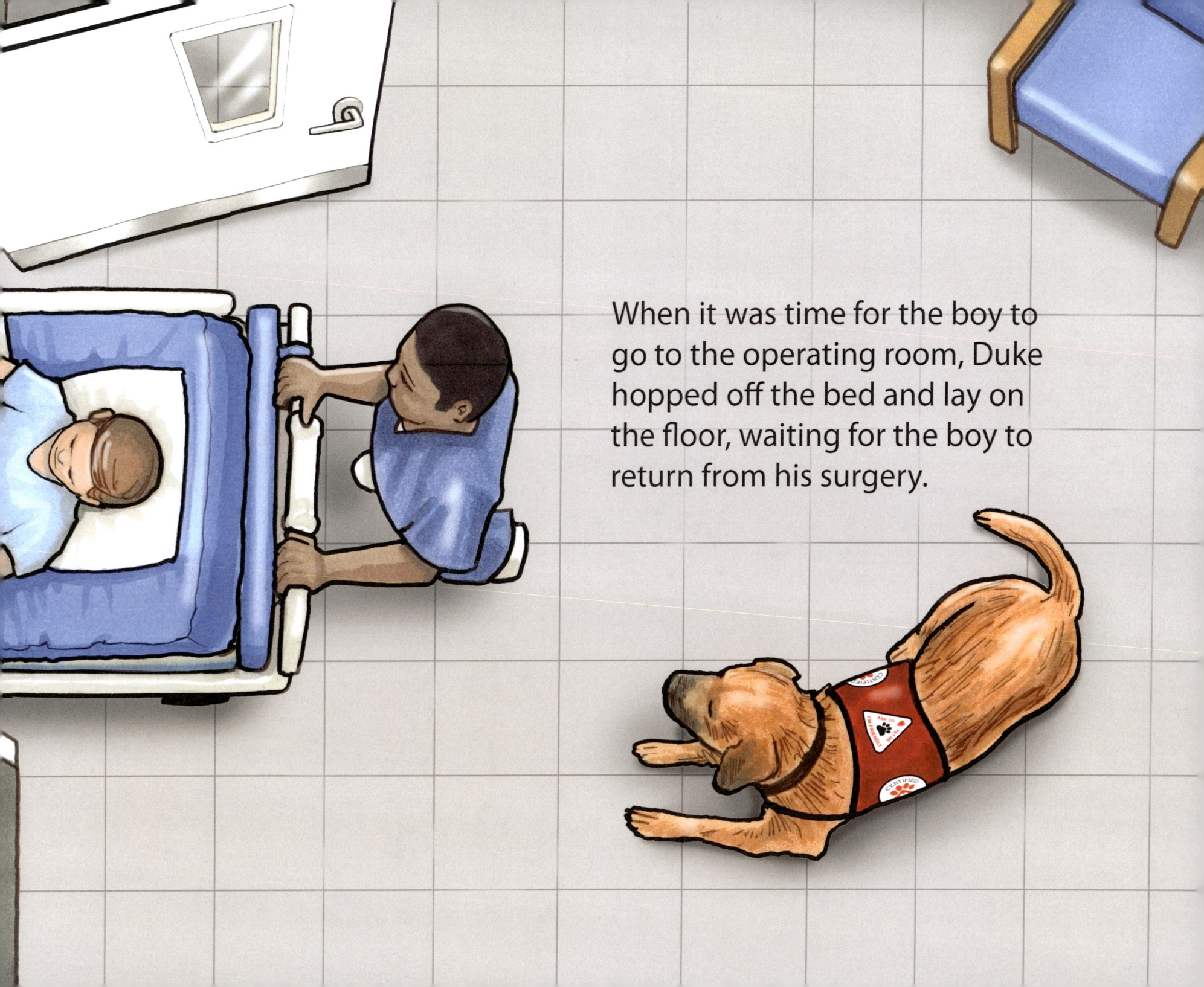

When it was time for the boy to go to the operating room, Duke hopped off the bed and lay on the floor, waiting for the boy to return from his surgery.

A few hours later, the boy returned to his hospital room. The operation had been successful!

Duke hopped back up on the bed and gave the boy a big kiss on the nose. The boy was so happy to see Duke. He wasn't sick or scared anymore.

Duke had done his job.

Duke always
remembered the
tough times in his life,
which made him want to help people
through their struggles.

As he walked down the hallway of the
hospital, he knew he had helped.

He felt
Ken's hand
on his head
before hearing
the words,
"Good boy,
Duke.
Good boy."

About the Author

Ken Brady is a professional dog trainer and motivational speaker. He lives with his family in Plymouth, Massachusetts and also spends a lot of his time hiking (with Duke) and skiing in the Stowe, Vermont area.